The Unnoticed

Short Poems on the Beauty We Forgot

Anmol Bhagat Khan

India | USA | UK

Made with ❤ on the BookLeaf Publishing Platform
www.bookleafpub.in
www.bookleafpub.com

Dedication

*To everyone who supported me—
thank you for making the
ordinary extraordinary.*

Preface

We often wait for life's big moments to bring us happiness, our achievements, celebrations, and milestones. But joy is not always found in grand gestures. Sometimes, it can be hidden in the smallest things: the rhythm of rain against the window, the way laughter lingers in a quiet room.

This book is my attempt to capture those fleeting, beautiful moments, ones we often overlook but later wish we had held onto just a little longer. Each poem offers a glimpse of the unnoticed magic of everyday life, a reminder that joy can be found in the simplest things if only we take a moment to see them.

At the end of this collection, you'll find two bonus poems. These pieces were turning points for me, the ones that made me believe I could truly write poetry. They are special not just because of the words on the page, but because of the confidence they gave me. I hope you find something special in them too.

Thank you for reading, for pausing, for noticing. May this book remind you that the ordinary is often extraordinary.

Acknowledgements

With heartfelt gratitude, I extend my deepest thanks to my parents, whose unwavering support, love, and encouragement have been my guiding light. Your belief in me has given me the strength to pursue my passion and turn my thoughts into words.

I would also like to thank Aarushi Ma'am, your guidance and kindness have shaped my journey in ways I cannot fully express. Thank you for inspiring me to grow as a writer and a person.

To my friends—Vishwara Aradhya, Arjuun, and Awani, thank you for standing by me, for your encouragement, laughter, and unwavering faith in me. Your presence has been a source of inspiration, and I am endlessly grateful for it.

To the BookLeaf Publishing Company, I am eternally grateful for this incredible opportunity to share my words with the world.

And to you, the reader, thank you for picking up this book and letting these words become a part of your journey. This book is not just a collection of poems but a testament to the love, belief, and support that surrounds me.

A Song Forgotten

Songs hold memories, and moments
Haunting us unexpectedly with voices low
Soft and sweet distance echoes
Tugging at the strings of a heart we know

Golden chords of summers spent
Rhythms wrapped in autumn's glow
Whispers in winters silence
Melting as spring winds blow

Every note, a thought unsaid
Pulling us through time and space
Calming hearts
A long lost, loved embrace

In chords of laughter, shadows play
Ebbing softly, like the tide's surrender
Dreams suspended in the air, a sway
Notes entwined, a fragile splendor

Familiar tunes, they hold us near
Whirling memories, both joy and fear
The heartstrings pull, the echoes rise
A silent language beneath the skies

In the melody's gentle, lapping waves
We find the fragments of our past
A bittersweet reminder of love and loss
A symphony that forever will last

And when the music fades away
The memories linger, night and day
A haunting refrain that echoes deep
A reminder of the secrets we keep.

The First Page

Today I bought a new journal
The fresh white first page stared at me
Too pure for the imperfections
Too blank for my thoughts to roam free

The lines stretched out like rivers
Waiting for creativity untold
Yet my hand hesitated, pen trembled
Afraid of the weight it would hold

What if my words weren't exquisite?
What if the ink left a stain?
Would the page still hold my secrets
Or whisper them back in refrain?

Then with a sigh I surrendered
Letting each letter flow true,
For even the messiest scribbles
Hold pieces of me shining through.

As I wrote, the page transformed
From pristine to a work of art
A tapestry of thoughts and emotions
A reflection of my imperfect heart

The ink stains became a map of my soul
A topography of my deepest thoughts
The scribbles and scratches, a symphony
A celebration of my unique self, brought.

Resilience

Resilience: I'd wondered what it meant
Until one cold morning, tired and spent
December the third, air sharp and still
The world wrapped in frost quiet and chill

My gaze fell on a fragile bloom
Rising from pavement defying the gloom
A tiny flower, golden and bright
Reaching for warmth, craving light

No shelter, no garden, no gentle embrace,
Yet there she stood, full of quiet grace
The wind may bend her, and the frost may bite
But still she stood and fought for the light

Her petals soft yet strong
A whispered lesson Id known all along

Resilience isn't loud or grand,
Its holding on with a strong heart and open hand.

In the harshest of conditions, she found a way
To push through the cold, to seize the day
A testament to the power of the soul
A reminder that resilience makes us whole

Shadows

In the morning, they whisper soft and slight
Slender in golden light
A gentle hush, a fleeting mark
Dancing between the morning sparks

By noon they shrink, hide and they fade
Tucked beneath the things they've made
Huddled close from the suns embrace
Lost within burning grace

Then evening spills in amber streams
Shadows grow like waking dreams
They reach they lean they softly sprawl
Climbing up twilights call

And when the night wraps up in rest
Shadows vanish lost suppressed
Yet wait for dawns call
To stretch along their track

But as the darkness reigns supreme
Their presence still, a subtle theme
A hidden world, a secret place
Where shadows weave their mystic space

And when the dawn breaks, slow and cold
They'll reappear, young, old
Stretching, yawning, taking their stand
Ready to dance, hand in hand.

Doodles

A heart, a star, a looping line
A thought half formed, a stray design
The margin fills and lesson fades
As ink escapes in quiet waves

A flower blooms a face appears
A mind that wanders but still hears
Not lost not gone just in between
A space where thought and daydream meet

The page meant for something more
but then again perhaps this is what its for
A tiny world a scribbled face
A fleeting breath of untamed space

Lost

The empty case, the silent grief,
A missing spark, a stolen thief.
You search and sigh, retrace the past,
But some small things slip loose too fast.

Then fingers brush against the shine,
A glimmer caught in folds of time.
Like fate had tucked it safe away,
Waiting for the right today.

You hold it close, a breath of relief,
A moment stitched with quiet belief.
Not all that's lost is lost for good,
Some things return when they should.

A tiny victory, a whisper bright,
A silver spark, a piece of light.
The weight of loss now softly mends
Some treasures know their way back home again.

In the crevices of memory and time,
Lost things await, like hidden rhymes.
They resurface, like a familiar face,
A reunion that fills the empty space.

The joy of recovery, a love so true,
A reminder that some losses are not anew.
For in the tapestry of life, we find
That lost threads can reweave, and love is aligned.

Photograph

The edges curl, the ink fades light,
Yet still, it holds the perfect night.
A frozen laugh, a golden glow,
A world that only you still know.

You touch the frame, as if to find,
A thread that ties you back in time.
The way you stood, the way they smiled,
The way the air had felt so wild.

No caption needed, no words remain,
Yet still, the memory speaks your name.
The echoes hum, the shadows call,
Like ghosts that dance against the wall.

And though the years have swept ahead,
That piece of time is never dead.
A glimpse, a glance, a step behind
A photo's magic never dies.

In faded hues, a story's told
Of moments lived, of memories old
The photograph, a window to the past
A bridge that spans the years so fast

The faces, the places, the love, the pain
All frozen in a single frame
A snapshot of a moment in time
A piece of history that's truly sublime.

Joy after sorrows

The storm has passed, the echoes fade,
Tears dry slow, like light through shade.
A hollow chest, a heavy sigh,
The weight of sorrow still sits high.

And then a sound, so soft, so small,
A chuckle breaks the grieving wall.
Like cracks in ice, like light through blinds,
A joy long lost, now redefined.

It catches you, it shakes your chest,
A sound so strange, yet feels like rest.
Not forced, not planned, just something true,
Like life reminding, "Hey, you're you."

The grief still lingers, that much is clear,
But laughter hums, still drawing near.
A bridge between what hurts and heals,
A breath that mends, a laugh that feels.

So let it rise, let sorrow bend,
For joy and pain both know no end.
And when they meet, just let them be
A heart can hold them equally.

The Last Slice

The box is light, the slices few,
You glance around, what will they do?
A single piece, a final bite,
A test of love, a stolen right.

Then comes the pause, the simple grin,
A gentle push, "Here, take it in."
No grand display, no speech so long,
Just kindness sung in actions strong.

They know you want it, know you crave,
Yet still, they choose the gift they gave.
A tiny thing, yet wrapped in care,
A love that says, "I know you're there."

For love is not in words alone,
But in the crumbs, in what is shown.
In little things we barely see,
That say, "You mean the world to me."

So take the slice, the final share,
A love so small, yet always rare.
A silent note, a perfect sign
To be thought of is so divine.

The Streetlight

A dim-lit path, a whispered glow,
A flicker faint, a light turned low.
You step beneath, the world stands still,
The lamp above bends to your will.

It blinks once twice a quiet game,
Like stars have learned to know your name.
A moment brief, a hidden sign,
A spark between your fate and time.

The street is empty, yet it hums,
Like something just for you has come.
A silent nod, a gentle spark,
A flame that dances in the dark.

You laugh, you move, you look behind,
But still, it flickers still, it shines.
Perhaps the world has tiny ways,
Of lighting up our lonely days.

In secret moments, hidden from sight
The universe conspires to guide our light
A whispered promise, a gentle hand
That leads us through life's uncertain plan

The lamp post stands, a sentinel true
A beacon in the darkness, shining through
A reminder that we're not alone
That even in the dark, a light is sown.

Lingering Laughter

It starts as a ripple, a breath, a spark,
A giggle that glows in the gathering dark.
It bounces off walls, it clings to the air,
A whisper of joy that lingers there.

It fades, but not for long,
It hums in echoes, soft yet strong.
A joke retold in the quiet night,
A memory wrapped in golden light.

It sneaks up on you days too late,
While pouring tea or locking a gate.
A sudden snort, a gasp for air,
Like laughter knows it's everywhere.

For some things end, but never leave,
They stay like warmth in winter's sleeve.
A joke, a grin, a fleeting sound,
Yet somehow, still, it sticks around.

The Last Page

The pages thin, the end draws near,
Yet something pulls, a touch of fear.
You slow your breath, you pace the read,
As if the words could halt their speed.

Then comes the line, the final thread,
A sentence strong, a thought well-spread.
It lingers there, like autumn's chill,
A whisper soft yet echoing still.

You close the book, yet hold it tight,
A weight now stitched into the night.
Not truly gone, not fully done,
An ending bright as rising sun.

In the silence, a echo stays,
A haunting memory of the final page's sway.
The characters, now ghosts in your mind,
Their stories woven, forever intertwined.

The book, now closed, its tale complete,
Leaves you with longing, a heart that skips a beat.
For in those pages, you found a friend,
A world that welcomed you, until the very end.

You Remember

A passing phrase, a glance, a note,
A tiny truth that someone wrote.
No grand display, no spoken cue,
Yet somehow, still, they always knew.

The way you like your coffee warm,
The song you hum when there's a storm.
The colour that you always wear,
The way you braid your wind-blown hair.

Not asked, not told, yet held with care,
Like secret things you didn't share.
A quiet love, a gift so small,
Yet somehow, still, it says it all.

For to be known in silent ways,
To be remembered, even days
Beyond the moment, past the scene,
Is proof of love, both soft and seen.

In the moments between words and sighs,
A deeper understanding meets the eyes.
A sense of connection, strong and true,
A bond that forms, without a word or two.

The memories linger, long after the fact,
A testament to the impact of a gentle act.
A small reminder, a quiet sign,
That someone noticed, and took the time.

Sunset

The colors creep in quietly,
blushes of pink, whispers of gold,
soft as the fading of a dream.

The sun lingers at the horizon,
dragging light behind it,
painting the sky with the last of its warmth.

Shadows stretch.
The clouds catch fire.
The world is wrapped in amber and rose,
as if the earth is holding its breath
before the darkness arrives.

And then
just for a moment
everything is perfect.

A masterpiece, drawn in light,
lasting only as long

as the sun allows.

The stars begin their twinkling waltz,
As night's soft veil descends,
a gentle romance.

The world is bathed in lunar glow,
A soothing serenade, a peaceful flow.

Cloud Dragon

The sky unfolds in strokes of blue,
And there it drifts a shape you knew.
A mighty beast with wings spread wide,
A dragon stitched into the sky.

Its tail unfurls, its body bends,
A fleeting friend the sky pretends.
A puff of white, a drifting gleam,
Yet somehow, still, it fuels a dream.

You point, you smile, you try to save
The shifting form, the shape it gave.
But clouds don't stay, they float, they run,
Like dreams that dance beneath the sun.

Still, in your mind, it stays aglow,
A dragon in the sky you know.
And though it fades, though winds rearrange,
The magic in the looking stays unchanged.

Warmth on a Cold Day

The wind bites.
It steals the breath from your lips,
turns your fingers stiff and pale,
curls cold around your bones.

And then- warmth.
A hand in yours,
solid, steady, alive.
Heat moves from skin to skin,
melting the frost between you.

It is a simple thing.
No grand gesture, no spoken word.
Just warmth, shared freely,
offered without a thought.

Yet somehow, it means everything.
A promise. A presence.
A touch that says:
I am here. I am real.

And in that warmth,
the cold loses its teeth.

The Perfect Pen

Some pens hesitate,
stutter across the page,
drag their feet through ink
like they do not want to be held.

But not this one.
This one glides,
smooth as a thought,
sharp as a promise.

It listens to your hand,
moves with your mind,
turns blankness into stories,
scratches silence into song.

Every letter is clean,
every word is bold,
as if the ink already knows
what it is meant to say.

You do not own this pen.
It owns you.
And together,
you make something real.

The First Raindrop

The air is thick with waiting,
clouds curled like fists in the sky.
The trees hold their breath,
the streets stand still,
a world on the edge of something vast.

Then, tap.
A drop lands on your sleeve,
light as a whisper,
heavy as a promise.
A signal, a start, a sigh.

The earth stirs.
Dust drinks deep.
The wind shifts its weight.
The sky is no longer holding back
it is letting go.

And suddenly, the hush is gone,
replaced by a rhythm, a roar, a rush.

The first drop never comes alone.
It is only the beginning.

The rain unwinds, a liquid thread,
Weaving life into the parched earth's bed.
Petals lift, and leaves unfold,
Drinking in the melody, young and old.

19. Drifting Off

Their voice a river, slow and deep,
A lullaby that pulls to sleep.
Each word dissolves, each sound unwinds,
A gentle hush, a peace that binds.

You fight the weight, you try to stay,
Yet sleep arrives, it will not wait.
Not boredom, no, not loss of care,
But comfort found in knowing they're there.

The steady rise, the softened tone,
The way their voice feels like home.
No fear of silence, no need to speak,
Just trust so deep it lets you sleep.

They do not mind, they do not stir,
They simply keep on speaking sure.
And when you wake, they're still the same
A presence wrapped in sound and name.

The gentle cadence, the reassuring tone,
A lullaby that's always known.
A voice that whispers, "You are safe,"
A presence that guards, a love that waits.

Unspoken Bond

No leash, no call, no name exchanged,
Yet here he sits, so close, unchanged.
A silent bond, a glance, a sigh,
No need to ask the reason why.

The world is loud, the streets are fast,
Yet he has found a place to last.
A simple press of fur to skin,
A warmth that lingers deep within.

No questions asked, no tales to tell,
Just trust that forms and sits so well.
A knowing gaze, a steady heart,
A friendship made in quiet parts.

The day moves on, the people blur,
Yet here he stays, a loyal stir.
For love is found in moments small,
A dog who sits that says it all.

In the midst of chaos, he finds a place,
A refuge from the noise, a steady face.
No need for words, no need to explain,
A simple presence, a calming refrain.

Flying Feather

It falls slowly,
a wisp of white against the sky,
spinning, swaying,
as if unsure where it should land.

Once, it belonged to something greater
a wing, a flight, a body that soared.
Now, it is free,
adrift on the breath of the world.

The wind plays with it,
tosses it high,
lets it fall,
carries it where it wants to go.

Does it miss what it was before?
Or is this weightless wandering
a new kind of belonging?

You watch it dance,
soft and silent,
and wonder
what would it be like to float like that?

To be a leaf on the breeze
a feather in flight,
To drift on the currents of air,
without a care or fight.

The world slows down, and you behold
The beauty of the fleeting, the fragile, the bold.
A single thread of white, a delicate design,
A moment's magic, a wonder that's truly divine.

Matching Outfits

A laugh erupts, a twin surprise,
A mirror flash in someone's eyes.
The same bright hue, the same soft thread,
As if your minds were loosely spread.

No plans were made, no words were said,
Yet here you stand in matching red.
A silent link, a woven tie,
A cosmic joke beneath the sky.

You grin, they grin, the world takes note,
Two echoes stitched in unseen coats.
A tiny sign, a thread so small,
Yet proof that souls can sync at all.

For some might say it's just a chance,
A silly fate, a passing glance.
But something hums when hearts align
A moment bright, a thread divine.

In the fabric of the universe's design,
A hidden pattern, a subtle shine.
A connection sparked, a moment's share,
Two kindred spirits, without a single care.

The world may see it as a simple sight,
But in that moment, something takes flight.
A bond is formed, a tie that's strong,
A memory etched, a moment that belongs.

Smells like Home

Not just perfume, not just the air,
But something woven deep in there.
A scent that lingers, soft yet strong,
Like memories stitched into a song.

You breathe them in, you close your eyes,
And suddenly, the years untie.
A hug from then, a place once known,
A childhood wrapped in undertones.

The way their sweater smells of peace,
Like quiet nights, like fallen leaves.
A touch of rain, a hint of dust,
The way the past still clings to us.

Not bottled scents, not store-bought sprays,
But something deep that always stays.
The way they smell is more than air
It's every time they've ever cared.

So when they pass, you breathe them in,
Like pages hold the ink within.
A love so simple, yet profound,
To smell like home is to be found.

In the folds of fabric, in the creases too,
Their scent remains, a memory or two.
A whiff of laughter, a hint of tears,
A fragrance that through the years appears.

The heart remembers what the mind forgets,
The scent of love, the smell of regrets.
A fragrance that transcends time and space,
A memory that holds a gentle face.

Bonus 1. Unseen, Unheard

What did I expect?
To leave a hemorrhage of violets wherever I walked?
No.

A lost son is called prodigal.
A lost daughter is just called lost.

No fanfare, no welcoming arms
For the daughter who strayed from charms
No forgiveness, no second chance
Just whispers, glances, and a dismissive dance

The son's return is celebrated with feasts
The daughter's with silence, and uneasy sleeps
Her path uncertain, and alone
While his paved with forgiveness, a home

I expected thorns, not roses sweet
For daughters who dare to stray from the beat
I expected shadows, not spotlights bright

For those who lose their way in endless night

But still I walk, through the dark and the pain
A lost daughter, with no name
No label to claim, no refuge to hide
Just the weight of expectations, inside

Bonus 2. Winters Solace

Bleed if you must,
Turn the world crimson with your fury,
Just don't abandon me,
In this unforgiving winter's grasp,
Where frost bites like a razor's edge,
And the wind howls with a mournful cry.

Linger a little longer,
For in your warmth, I find solace,
A fleeting respite from the ache,
A gentle thaw to frozen bones,

Stay,
Melt the snow that blinds and silences,
Let out rage and sorrow,
Fuel a flame that guides through winter's night.